Abortion Legislation in Europe

Armenia • Austria • Belgium • Czech Republic
Denmark • Finland • France • Germany
Great Britain • Iceland • Ireland
Italy • Latvia • Netherlands
Norway • Poland • Portugal
Russian Federation • Spain
Sweden • Switzerland
Ukraine

January 2015

Contents

Comparative Summary

Luis Acosta
Acting Chief, Foreign, Comparative, and International Law Division II

This report summarizing laws on abortion in selected European countries shows diverse approaches to the regulation of abortion in Europe.

A majority of the surveyed countries allow abortion upon the woman's request in the early weeks of pregnancy, and allow abortion under specified circumstances in later periods. Some countries impose a waiting period of a certain number of days following counseling. Some require consultation with medical personnel before an abortion may be performed. Several countries require that medical personnel certify the abortion is for a reason permitted by law. The most restrictive country surveyed here, Ireland, allows abortion only when there is a real and substantial risk to the woman's life.

Map 1 (below) visually depicts by country the availability of abortion during the initial weeks of pregnancy in the countries surveyed. Map 2 shows the time limits for abortion upon the woman's request in the applicable countries.

At the supranational level, all of the countries surveyed are members of the European Convention on Human Rights.[1] The European Court of Human Rights (ECtHR), which hears allegations of violations of the Convention, has issued some decisions on procedural aspects of abortion access. For example, in *Open Door Counselling v. Ireland*, the ECtHR ruled that an injunction by an Irish court prohibiting family planning clinics from informing patients of the availability of abortion in England violated the right to freedom of information and expression found in article 10 of the Convention.[2] In *Tysiac v. Poland*, the ECtHR ruled that where doctors failed to certify the availability of an abortion to a woman whose continued pregnancy threatened her health, the government's failure to establish a procedure for determining whether an abortion was lawful violated the right to respect for private life under article 8 of the Convention.[3] Similarly, in *A, B & C v. Ireland*, the ECtHR ruled that Ireland's failure to provide a mechanism for establishing whether a woman was lawfully entitled to an abortion on health grounds violated article 8 of the Convention.[4]

---

[1] Convention for the Protection of Human Rights and Fundamental Freedoms, Nov. 4, 1950, 213 U.N.T.S. 222, http://conventions.coe.int/Treaty/en/Treaties/Html/005.htm (updated to June 1, 2010). All forty-seven Member States of the Council of Europe are members of this Convention. *A Convention to Protect Your Rights and Liberties*, COUNCIL OF EUROPE, http://human-rights-convention.org/ (last visited Jan. 20, 2015).

[2] Open Door Counselling, Ltd. v. Ireland, 15 E.H.R.R. 244 (1993).

[3] Tysiac v. Poland, App. No. 5410/03, ¶¶ 124, 125 (2007), http://hudoc.echr.coe.int/sites/eng/pages/search.aspx?i=001-79812.

[4] A, B & C v. Ireland, App. No. 25579/05, ¶¶ 264–268 (2010), http://hudoc.echr.coe.int/sites/eng/pages/search.aspx?i=001-102332.

Map 1

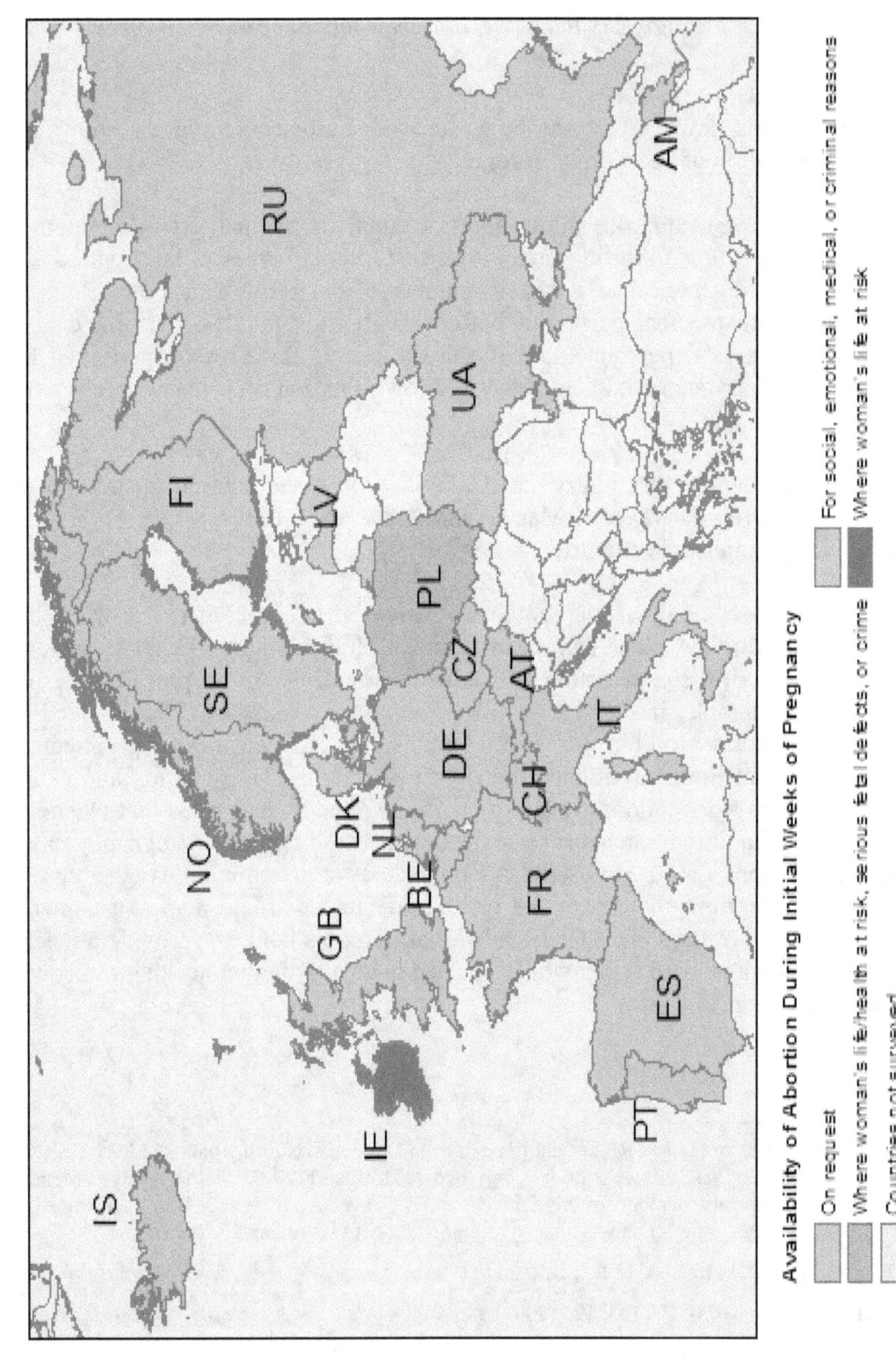

Availability of Abortion During Initial Weeks of Pregnancy

- On request
- Where woman's life/health at risk, serious fetal defects, or crime
- Countries not surveyed
- For social, emotional, medical, or criminal reasons
- Where woman's life at risk

Source: Created by the Law Library of Congress based on country-specific information included in this report.

Map 2

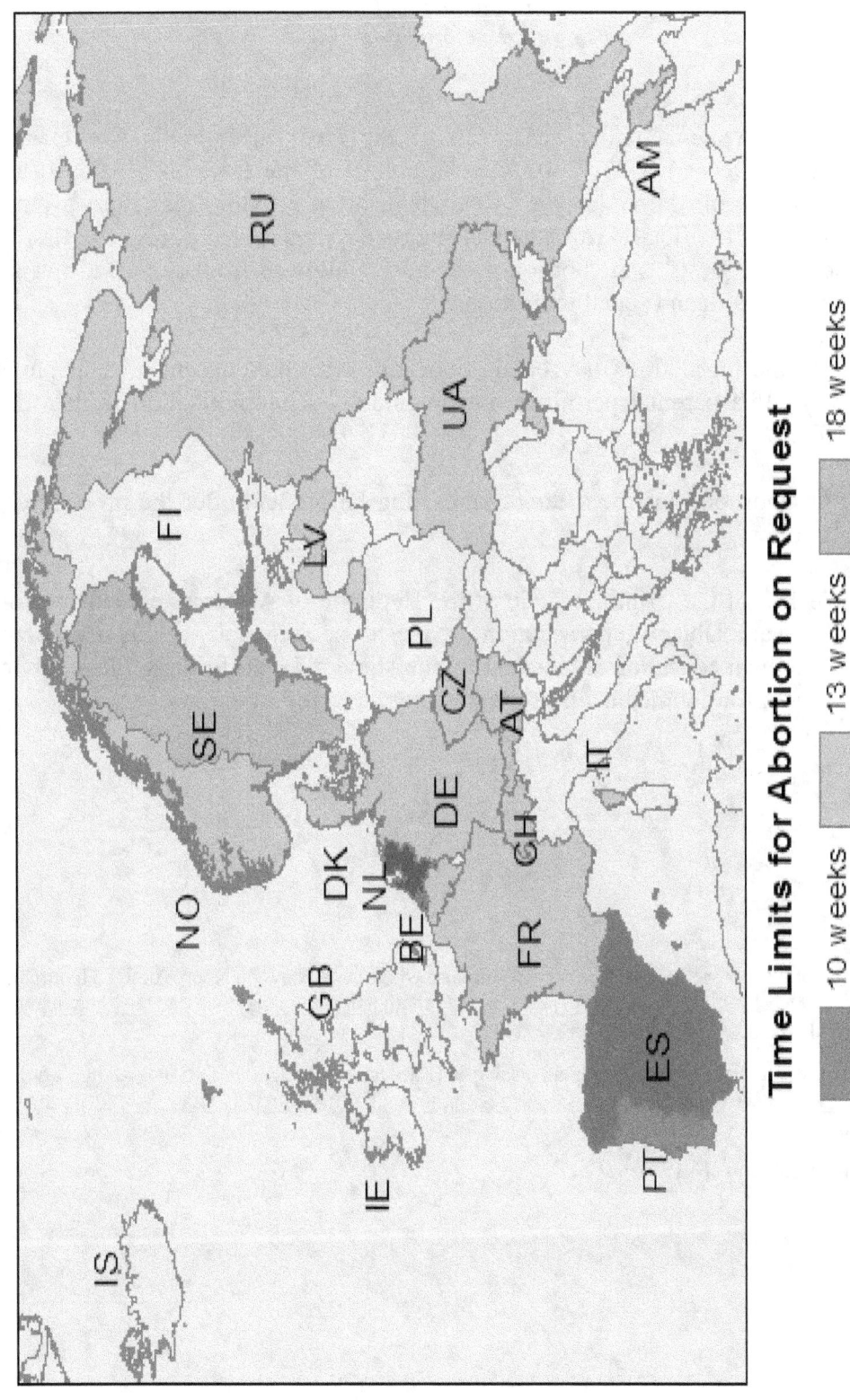

Time Limits for Abortion on Request

10 weeks	13 weeks
12 weeks	14 weeks
18 weeks	
22 weeks	

Source: Created by the Law Library of Congress based on country-specific information included in this report. Subset of Map 1 countries that allow abortion "on request." Time periods reflected are approximate. For example, Austrian law specifies "three months," which was rounded to "13 weeks" on this map for ease of comparison.

Armenia

Olena Yatsunska-Poff
Foreign Law Consultant

Abortions are legal in Armenia under article 10 of the Law on Reproductive Health and Reproductive Rights of December 11, 2002,[1] and article 9 of the Law on Medical Care and Services to the Population of March 4, 1996.[2] This legislation provides that every woman has the right to an abortion.[3] Artificial termination of pregnancy is allowed during the first twelve weeks of pregnancy on request.[4] An abortion procedure is allowed from twelve to twenty-two weeks of pregnancy on health and social indications.[5]

Minors, according to the legislation, may obtain abortions with the consent of their parents or legal representatives. If a parental permit is not obtainable, an authorization from a medical commission is required.[6]

A woman having an abortion must be offered counseling before and after the procedure but is not required to accept it.[7]

According to article 122 of the Criminal Code of the Republic of Armenia, persons performing unauthorized abortions are subject to prosecution.[8] Medical personnel as well as people with no appropriate, higher medical education are subject to punishment for performing illegal abortions, although the punishment for nonmedical personnel is more severe.[9]

---

[1] Zakon o Reproduktivnom Zdorovie I Reproduktivnykh Pravakh Cheloveka [Law on Reproductive Health and Reproductive Rights] of Dec.11, 2002, http://www.parliament.am/legislation.php?sel=show&ID=1339&lang=rus (official publication; in Russian).

[2] Zakon o Meditsinskoy Pomoshchi, Obsluzhivaniia Naseleniia [Law on Medical Care, Services to the Population] of March 4, 1996, http://www.moh.am/?section=static_pages/index&id=235&subID=59&lang=ru (official publication; in Russian).

[3] Law on Reproductive Health art. 10.1.

[4] *Id.* art. 10.2.

[5] *Id.* art. 10.3.

[6] *Id.* art. 10.4.

[7] *Id.* art. 10.5.

[8] CRIMINAL CODE OF THE REPUBLIC OF ARMENIA art. 122, *available at* http://www.legislationline.org/documents/section/criminal-codes (in English translation).

[9] *Id.* art. 122.2.

Austria

Wendy Zeldin
Senior Legal Research Analyst

Abortion in Austria is governed by the Federal Law of 23 January 1974 (in force January 1, 1975),[1] through which provisions on abortion were adopted in the Criminal Code. Abortions are available on request by a pregnant woman for up to three months from completed implantation. They must be performed in public hospitals by a physician after a medical consultation with the patient,[2] following the completion of examinations and certain required tests—namely, a blood group and Rhesus factor test, ultrasound examination, HIV test, and hepatitis test.[3]

Abortions may also be performed without criminal liability after that period in order to avert serious danger to the life, physical health, or mental health of the pregnant woman; if serious danger exists of physical or mental impairment to the fetus; if the woman is under fourteen years of age; or if an abortion is the only way of averting immediate danger to the woman's life and no medical aid is available at the time.[4]

---

[1] BUNDESGESETZ VOM 23. JÄNNER 1974 ÜBER DIE MIT GERICHTLICHER STRAFE BEDROHTEN HANDLUNGEN (STRAFGESETZBUCH [STGB]) [FEDERAL LAW OF 23 JANUARY 1974 ON PUNISHABLE ACTS (PENAL CODE [STGB]) (in force on Jan. 1, 1975, as last amended by BUNDESGESETZBLATT [BGBL] I Nr. 106/214, Dec. 29, 2014, Part I, No. 1974/60, Stück 21, pp. 641–92, https://www.ris.bka.gv.at/GeltendeFassung.wxe?Abfrage=Bundesnormen&Gesetzesnummer=10002296. Sections 96, 97, and 98 of the Penal Code are on abortion. For an English translation of the provisions, see Austria. Federal Law of 23 January 1974, http://cyber.law.harvard.edu/population/abortion/Austria.abo.htm (last visited Jan. 13, 2015).

[2] PENAL CODE § 97(1)1; Österreichische Gesellschaft für Familienplanung (ÖGF), *Austria*, *in* INTERNATIONAL PLANNED PARENTHOOD FEDERATION [IPPF] EUROPEAN NETWORK, ABORTION LEGISLATION IN EUROPE 11 (updated Jan. 2012), http://www.ippfen.org/sites/default/files/ Final_Abortion%20legislation_September2012.pdf.

[3] ÖGF, *supra* note 2.

[4] *Id.*; PENAL CODE §§ 97(1)2 & 97(1)3.

Belgium

Nicolas Boring
Foreign Law Specialist

The principal rules on abortion in Belgium are found in the Penal Code.[1] Belgian law authorizes women to obtain an abortion when they are feeling "distress" because of their pregnancy.[2] The Code does not define "distress" but it seems that the term is interpreted in a very broad manner. Indeed, it appears that not feeling ready for a child is enough to qualify as "distress" under the law.[3]

Abortions in Belgium must be done before the end of the twelfth week after conception, and must be done by a medical doctor.[4] Before performing the abortion, the doctor must inform the patient of the medical risks related to abortion, and must also inform her of options that would be available to her if she chose not to have an abortion, such as adoption.[5] Furthermore, Belgian law requires a six-day waiting period after the first consultation, before an abortion may be legally performed.[6]

After the end of the twelfth week, an abortion is only legal if the pregnancy would seriously endanger the woman's health, or if it is certain that the child would be born with a particularly serious health problem that is untreatable at the time of the diagnosis. The doctor must make this determination with the concurrence of another doctor.[7]

No health care professional may be compelled to participate in an abortion. If a doctor refuses to perform an abortion, however, he/she must inform the patient of this refusal during the first consultation.[8]

---

[1] CODE PÉNAL [PENAL CODE], http://www.ejustice.just.fgov.be/cgi_loi/change_lg.pl?language=fr&la=F&table_name=loi&cn=1867060801.

[2] *Id.* art. 350.

[3] SÉNAT ET CHAMBRE DES REPRÉSENTANTS DE BELGIQUE [SENATE AND CHAMBER OF REPRESENTATIVES OF BELGIUM], RAPPORT DE LA COMMISSION NATIONALE D'ÉVALUATION DE LA LOI DU 3 AVRIL 1990 RELATIVE À L'INTERRUPTION DE GROSSESSE [REPORT OF THE NATIONAL COMMISSION FOR THE EVALUATION OF THE LAW OF APRIL 3, 1990, REGARDING PREGNANCY INTERRUPTION] 60 (Aug. 27, 2012), http://www.lachambre.be/FLWB/PDF/53/2399/53K2399001.pdf.

[4] CODE PÉNAL art. 350(1°).

[5] *Id.* art. 350(2°).

[6] *Id.* art. 350(3°).

[7] *Id.* art. 350(4°).

[8] *Id.* art. 350(6°).

Czech Republic

Olena Yatsunska-Poff
Foreign Law Consultant

The artificial termination of pregnancy is legal in the Czech Republic and is regulated under the Law on Abortion of October 20, 1986,[1] and the Notification of the Ministry of Health of the Czechoslovak Socialist Republic of November 7, 1986 (last amended September 8, 1992) on Implementation of the Law on Abortion.[2]

The Law establishes the basic principle that an abortion procedure can be performed for any reason upon a woman's written request submitted to a gynecologist employed by a health establishment serving her place of permanent residence, place of work, or school if the pregnancy has not passed the twelfth week. However, the request may be denied if the gynecologist determines that an abortion would be detrimental to the woman's health. During the same twelve-week period, an abortion can be performed on health grounds upon medical recommendation with the woman's approval; on the woman's initiative if her life or health or the healthy development of the fetus are endangered, or if fetal development manifests genetic abnormalities;[3] or when the pregnancy results from rape or another sexual crime.[4]

After the twelfth week of pregnancy, an abortion can be performed only if the life of the woman is threatened or when it is proven that the fetus is severely damaged or incapable of life.[5] If there are serious medical indications (genetic grounds), the procedure can be carried out up to twenty-four weeks.[6]

The 1986 Ministry of Health Notification includes the list of illnesses that can threaten the life and health of a pregnant woman. Among them are diseases of the heart and vascular system; pulmonary and heart illnesses; blood formation pathologies; cancerous tumors; tuberculosis; and some neurological, genetic, and mental diseases.[7]

---

[1] Zákon České Národní Rady o Umělém Přerušení Těhotenství [Law of the Czech National Council on Abortion (hereinafter Law on Abortion)] of Oct. 20, 1986, SBIRKA ZAKONU (official gazette) No. 66/1986 Sb., http://www.pravnipredpisy.cz/predpisy/ZAKONY/1986/066986/Sb_066986_------_.php#Z%C1KON%20 %C8ESK%C9/////%A7%204 (in Czech).

[2] Vyhláška Ministerstva Zdravotnictví České Socialistické Republiky Kterou Se Provádí Zákon České Národní Rady No.66/1986 Sb., o Umělém Přerušení Těhotenství [Notification of the Ministry of Health of the Czech Socialist Republic on the Implementation of Law No. 66/1986 Sb. on Abortion], Nov. 7, 1986, SBIRKA ZAKONU No. 75/1986 Sb., http://www.cgps.cz/cgps/doc/75_1986_Sb.txt (in Czech).

[3] Law on Abortion §§ 4, 5.

[4] Notification of the Ministry of Health, *supra* note 2, § 1.3.

[5] *Id.* § 2.1.

[6] *Id.* § 2.2.

[7] *Id.*

If the woman seeking an abortion has not reached the age of sixteen, the consent of her parent, guardian, or legal representative is required.[8]

An unauthorized abortion is prosecuted under article 227 of the Criminal Code of the Czech Republic. A person who assists a pregnant woman or induces her to interrupt her pregnancy by herself or asks or allows someone else to interrupt her pregnancy in a manner other than authorized by law must be sentenced to a term of imprisonment of up to one year.[9]

---

[8] Law on Abortion § 6.1.

[9] Criminal Code of the Czech Republic art. 227, SBIRKA ZAKONU No. 140/1961, *available at* http://www.coe.int/ t/dlapil/codexter/Source/country_profiles/legislation/CT%20Legislation%20-%20Czech%20Republic%20Criminal %20Code.pdf (in English translation).

Denmark

Elin Hofverberg
Foreign Law Research Consultant

Abortion is regulated in chapter 25 of Denmark's Health Act.[1] Abortions at the woman's request may be carried out before week twelve of the pregnancy without prior permission.[2] Following week twelve abortions may only be carried out if

> 1) the pregnancy, delivery or care of the child would cause risk to the expectant mother's health as a result of physical or psychological illness, depression or weakness that follows from her life situation;
>
> 2) the mother became pregnant as a result of [certain criminalized sexual offenses, such as rape, statutory rape, incest, etc.];
>
> 3) there is a great risk that the child will suffer from a serious disease as a result of a genetic predisposition or harmful effects suffered during the pregnancy;
>
> 4) the expectant mother, as a result of physical or psychological illness or other weakness, cannot provide the child with the required care;
>
> 5) the mother, because of youth or immaturity, will be unable to adequately care for the child; or
>
> 6) the pregnancy, delivery, or care of the child can be expected to cause such a serious and unavoidable burden on the mother that it is in her interests or the interests of maintaining her home or caring for the family's other children that the pregnancy be terminated. Consideration shall be given to the woman's age, employment, and personal circumstances as well as the family's living situation and financial circumstances from a holistic perspective.[3]

However, abortions may always be carried out if continuing the pregnancy is a threat to the life or health of the woman.[4] The abortion of a fetus that can survive outside the womb may be carried out only if there is risk that the child will contract a serious disease or emotional illness as a result of either genetics or illness while in the womb.[5]

A request for an abortion must be presented by the woman herself;[6] if she is under the age of eighteen, she must have the consent of her legal guardian.[7] However, the Council for Abortion

---

[1] Sundhedsloven, LBK nr. 1202 af 14/11/2014, https://www.retsinformation.dk/forms/r0710.aspx?id=152710#Kap25.

[2] *Id.* art. 92.

[3] *Id.* art. 94, para. 1, items 1–6.

[4] *Id.* art. 93.

[5] *Id.* art. 94, para. 3.

[6] *Id.* art. 98.

[7] *Id.* art. 99, para. 1.

and Sterilization may determine that approval from the legal guardian is not necessary.[8] The woman requesting the abortion must be provided with medical information[9] and a counseling session before and after the procedure.[10]

Following week twelve, only doctors at regional hospitals may terminate a pregnancy.[11] Doctors, nurses, and other hospital personnel may decline to participate in abortions.[12]

---

[8] *Id.* paras. 2, 3.

[9] *Id.* art. 100, para. 3.

[10] *Id.* para. 5.

[11] *Id.* art. 101.

[12] *Id.* art. 102.

Finland

Elin Hofverberg
Foreign Law Research Consultant

Abortion in Finland is regulated by the Act on Termination of Pregnancy.[1] Abortions may be performed

1) when continuing the pregnancy or delivery would constitute a threat to the mother's life or health because of the mother's illness, physical disability, or weakness;

2) when the delivery and care of the child would cause considerable burden on the mother with regard to her and her family's living situation and other circumstances;

3) when the pregnancy was the result of criminal acts listed in the Criminal Code [such as incest or rape];

4) if the mother at the time of conception had not turned seventeen, or had turned forty and had already given birth to four children;

5) when there is cause to suspect that the child would become mentally challenged, [or] is suffering from or may later develop a severe illness or physical disability; or

6) when either of the parents has an illness that seriously limits his or her capability to care for the child.[2]

An abortion for the aforementioned reasons requires the consent of two medical physicians or, when necessary because of an illness of the child, the consent of the National Authority for Medicolegal Affairs.[3] Abortions must be performed by a licensed physician either at a specially designated abortion hospital or outside a hospital if the woman's health requires immediate action.[4]

Abortions must be performed as early in the pregnancy as possible and may not be carried out after week twenty. An abortion may not be carried out because of a previously known illness of the woman after week twelve of the pregnancy.[5] However, an abortion performed because of the health of the child may be performed until week twenty-four.[6]

---

[1] Lag om avbrytande av havandeskap [Act on Termination of Pregnancy] 24.3.1970/239, as amended, available on the Finlex website (maintained in Finnish and Swedish in part by the Finnish Ministry of Justice), http://www. finlex.fi/sv/laki/ajantasa/1970/19700239?search%5Btype%5D=pika&search%5Bpika%5D=abort (in Swedish).

[2] *Id.* art. 1.

[3] *Id.* art. 6.

[4] *Id.* arts. 8, 9.

[5] *Id.* art. 5.

[6] *Id.* art. 5 a.

Abortions are performed at the request of the woman,[7] but she must first be advised of the effects of the abortion.[8] However, the father may be given the opportunity to present his views prior to the decision to terminate the pregnancy, but only if there are special reasons that warrant doing so.[9]

A person who gets an abortion in violation of the Act may be fined.[10]

---

[7] *Id.* art. 1.

[8] *Id.* art. 4.

[9] *Id.* art. 7, para. 1.

[10] *Id.* art. 13.

France

Nicolas Boring
Foreign Law Specialist

Abortion was initially legalized in France by Loi No. 75-17 du 17 janvier 1975 relative à l'interruption volontaire de la grossesse (Law No. 75-17 of January 1975 Regarding Voluntary Interruption of Pregnancy).[1] Most current rules on abortion are found in the Public Health Code.[2]

French law authorizes women to obtain an abortion until the end of the twelfth week of pregnancy.[3] After the twelfth week of pregnancy, French law only permits an abortion if two doctors from a multidisciplinary team confirm, after consulting with the rest of their team, that carrying the pregnancy to term would seriously endanger the woman's health, or that there is a strong probability that the child would be born with particularly serious health problems that are untreatable at the time of the diagnosis.[4]

All abortions must be performed by a medical doctor.[5] When a pregnant woman comes to a doctor to ask for an abortion, the latter must inform her during the first consultation about the medical and surgical methods of abortion, and about the risks and potential side-effects.[6] French law also provides that the patient be offered a consultation with a marriage counselor, family planning counselor, or social services, both before and after the abortion.[7] An adult woman is free to accept or decline these offers of consultation, but the pre-abortion consultation is mandatory for unemancipated minors.[8]

Any health care professional may refuse to participate in an abortion. If a doctor refuses to perform an abortion, however, he/she must give the patient the names of other doctors who would be able to perform an abortion.[9]

---

[1] Loi No. 75-17 du 17 janvier 1975 relative à l'interruption volontaire de la grossesse [Law No. 75-17 of January 17, 1975, Regarding Voluntary Interruption of Pregnancy], JOURNAL OFFICIEL DE LA RÉPUBLIQUE FRANÇAISE [J.O.] [OFFICIAL GAZETTE OF FRANCE], Jan. 18, 1975, p. 739, http://www.legifrance.gouv.fr/jopdf/common/jo_pdf. jsp?numJO=0&dateJO=19750118&numTexte=&pageDebut=00739&pageFin=00741.

[2] CODE DE LA SANTÉ PUBLIQUE [PUBLIC HEALTH CODE], http://www.legifrance.gouv.fr/affichCode.do; jsessionid=ED741182F75ACC70E37A5FC12AA0CF98.tpdjo02v_1?cidTexte=LEGITEXT000006072665&dateTe xte=20150115.

[3] *Id.* art. L2212-1.

[4] *Id.* art. L2213-1.

[5] *Id.* art. L2212-2.

[6] *Id.* art. L2212-3.

[7] *Id.* art. L2212-4.

[8] *Id.*

[9] *Id.* art. L2212-8.

Germany

Wendy Zeldin
Senior Legal Research Analyst

Under the German Penal Code, termination of pregnancy (*Schwangerschaftsabbruch*) or abortion (*Abtreibung*) is unlawful but permitted on demand under certain conditions and also on medical and criminal grounds when requested by the pregnant woman.

An abortion may be performed by a physician at the request of a pregnant woman if she presents to the physician a certificate indicating that she obtained counseling at least three days before the operation and not more than twelve weeks have elapsed since conception.[1] However, the Code also provides for an upper limit of twenty-two weeks for an abortion when the pregnant woman has had counseling and a court order discharges the person who terminates the pregnancy because the woman was "in exceptional distress at the time of the operation."[2]

An abortion may be performed by a physician with the consent of the pregnant woman if it is medically necessary to prevent danger to her life or grave injury to her physical or mental health "and if the danger cannot reasonably be averted in another way from her point of view," taking into consideration the woman's present and future living conditions.[3] In such instances, there is a gestational limit of not more that twenty-two weeks of pregnancy.[4]

An abortion may be performed on criminal grounds with the pregnant woman's consent, within twelve weeks following conception, where, based on medical opinion, "there is strong reason to support the assumption that the pregnancy was caused by [a criminal] act" (e.g., child abuse, sexual assault, rape).[5]

In the case of medical or criminal grounds for an abortion, an independent doctor must verify that such grounds exist and provide a medical certificate to that effect, and the certifying doctor may not perform the operation.[6]

---

[1] STRAFGESETZBUCH [STGB] [PENAL CODE], Nov. 13, 1998, BUNDESGESETZBLATT [BGBL.] I at 3322, *last amended by* Gesetz [Law], Oct. 2, 2009, BGBL. I at 3214, § 218a(1), http://www.gesetze-im-internet.de/englisch_stgb/index.html (toggle the flag icon for the text of the Code in German, as last amended Apr. 23, 2014, and scroll down to relevant article).

[2] *Id.* § 218(4).

[3] *Id.* § 218a(2).

[4] *Id.* § 218a(4); *see also Termination of Pregnancy and Abortion in Germany*, ANGLOINFO, http://berlin.angloinfo.com/information/health_care/pregnancy-birth/termination-abortion/ (last visited Jan. 15, 2015).

[5] STGB § 218a(3). This provision refers to the unlawful acts set forth under §§ 176–179 of the Code.

[6] ANGLOINFO, *supra* note 4.

Great Britain

Clare Feikert-Ahalt
Senior Foreign Law Specialist

Abortions are permitted in Great Britain in specific circumstances. The Abortion Act 1967 establishes the framework for lawful abortions. This Act provides that medical termination of pregnancy is lawful up to the twenty-fourth week of pregnancy.[1] Section 1 of the Act requires the procedure to be performed by a registered medical practitioner, and only if two registered medical practitioners form an opinion in good faith that the pregnancy has not exceeded the twenty-fourth week and that the continuation of the pregnancy would involve a risk to the physical or mental health of the pregnant woman or any of her existing children. There is no time limit for an abortion if there is a substantial risk that, if the child were born, it would suffer from physical or mental abnormalities that would result in a serious handicap, if the abortion would prevent grave permanent injury to the physical or mental health of the pregnant woman, or if the continuation of the pregnancy would involve risk to the life of the pregnant woman. In these instances, two medical practitioners must agree that these circumstances exist.[2]

The assessment of the mental health of the pregnant woman may take into account the woman's "actual or reasonably foreseeable environment."[3] There is no requirement in law that the medical practitioners examine the woman in person; however, guidance from the Department of Health states that "both doctors should ensure that they have considered sufficient information specific to the woman seeking a termination to be able to assess whether the woman satisfies one of the lawful grounds under the Abortion Act."[4]

The abortion procedure must take place in a hospital or other place approved by the Secretary of State.[5] Registered medical practitioners may also terminate pregnancies without an additional opinion of another practitioner in emergency situations. An emergency situation exists where the medical practitioner believes, in good faith, that the termination is immediately necessary to save the life or prevent permanent, grave injury to the physical or mental health of the pregnant woman.[6]

There are no waiting periods required by law for an abortion to occur. However, as Great Britain has socialized health care, there can be wait times due to patient demand. The National

---

[1] Abortion Act, 1967, c. 87, § 1, http://www.legislation.gov.uk/ukpga/1967/87/section/1.

[2] *Id.*

[3] *Id.* § 1(2).

[4] DEPARTMENT OF HEALTH, GUIDANCE IN RELATION TO THE REQUIREMENTS OF THE ABORTION ACT 1967, ¶ 12 (May 2014), https://www.gov.uk/government/uploads/system/uploads/attachment_data/file/313459/20140509_-_Abortion_Guidance_Document.pdf.

[5] Abortion Act, 1967, c. 87, § 1(3).

[6] *Id.* § 1(4).

Health Service has stated that patients should generally not have to wait longer than two weeks from the date of the initial appointment to the date of the procedure.[7]

The Offences Against the Person Act 1861 provides that it is a criminal offense to unlawfully cause a miscarriage.[8] The Infant Life (Preservation) Act 1929 further provides for the offense of intentionally killing a fetus that is capable of being born alive.[9]

---

[7] *Abortion: Where to Go*, NHS CHOICES, http://www.nhs.uk/Livewell/Sexualhealth/Pages/Abortionyouroptions.aspx (last visited Jan. 14, 2015).

[8] Offences Against the Person Act, 1861, 24 & 25 Vict., c. 100, § 58, http://www.legislation.gov.uk/ukpga/Vict/24-25/100/contents.

[9] Infant Life (Preservation) Act, 1929, 19 & 20 Geo., c. 34, § 1, http://www.legislation.gov.uk/ukpga/Geo5/19-20/34/section/1.

Iceland

Elin Hofverberg
Foreign law Research Consultant

Abortion in Iceland is regulated by the Act on Counselling and Education Regarding Sex and Childbirth and on Abortion and Sterilization Procedures.[1]   Article 9 of that Act lists the circumstances in which an abortion may be performed:

> Abortion is permitted:
> 1.   Social factors: When the woman and her closest family may be deemed unable to cope with the pregnancy and birth of a child, due to social circumstances beyond their control. Under such circumstances the following shall be taken into account:
>   a.   Whether the woman has given birth to a large number of children in a short time, and whether a short time has passed since the most recent birth.
>   b.   Whether the woman lives in poor home conditions due to having a large family of young children or due to serious ill-health of others in the home.
>   c.   Whether the woman is, due to young age or immaturity, incapable of caring adequately for the child.
>   d.   Other circumstances fully equivalent to those specified above.
> 2.   Medical factors:
>   a.   When the woman's health, physical or mental, may be deemed to be at risk from continued pregnancy and childbirth.
>   b.   When the child the woman is carrying may be deemed to be at risk of being born malformed, or with some serious disease, due to genetic factors or fetal damage.
>   c.   When an illness, physical or mental, greatly diminishes the ability of a woman or man to care for a child and bring him/her up.
> 3.   When a woman has been raped, or has become pregnant as a result of some other criminal act.[2]

Abortions must, if possible, be performed before week twelve of the pregnancy.[3]   Following week sixteen, abortions may be performed only because of the health of the woman or the fetus.[4]

The woman must sign the request for an abortion.   If she is less than sixteen years old, the request must also be signed by her parents except in special circumstances.[5]   The father of the fetus should also sign the request, although he is not required to do so.[6]

---

[1] Lög um ráðgjöf og fræðslu varðandi kynlíf og barneignir og um fóstureyðingar og ófrjósemisaðgerðir, 1975 nr. 25 22. maí, http://www.althingi.is/lagas/nuna/1975025.html.

[2] Act on Counselling and Education Regarding Sex and Childbirth and on Abortion and Sterilisation Procedures, No. 25/1975, *as amended by* Act No. 82/1998, No. 162/2010 and No. 126/2011, art. 9, http://eng.velferdarraduneyti. is/media/acrobat-enskar_sidur/Act_on_counselling_and_instruction_etc_No_25_1975_as_amended.pdf (unofficial English translation).

[3] *Id.* art. 10.

[4] *Id.*

[5] *Id.* art. 13.

According to the Law, abortions may be performed only by physicians in hospitals that have been specially recognized for the purpose by the Minister of Welfare and that have a specialist in gynecology or general surgery on the staff.[7] Two physicians or a physician and a social worker must make a written report supporting the abortion before it is performed.[8]

A woman seeking an abortion must be provided with information on medical assistance, pregnancy tests, counseling and support, social assistance, and assistance with the abortion request, as well as a referral to the hospital.[9] In addition, she must be provided with information on the medical risks involved in an abortion and available societal support should she choose to forego an abortion.[10]

Physicians violating the abortion regulations may be fined or imprisoned for up to two years. A nonphysician who performs an abortion may be imprisoned for up to four years.[11]

---

[6] *Id.*

[7] *Id.* art. 15.

[8] *Id.* art. 11.

[9] *Id.* art. 6.

[10] *Id.* art. 12.

[11] *Id.* art. 31.

Ireland

Clare Feikert-Ahalt
Senior Foreign Law Specialist

The Republic of Ireland has a highly restrictive approach to abortion, only permitting it in very limited circumstances when the life of the woman is at risk.[1] Article 40.3.3 of the Irish Constitution acknowledges unborn children as having the right to life, specifically stating as follows:

> The State acknowledges the right to life of the unborn and, with due regard to the equal right to life of the mother, guarantees in its laws to respect, and, as far as practicable, by its laws to defend and vindicate that right.[2]

The Supreme Court has interpreted this article as prohibiting abortion in Ireland, with the exception of cases where it can be established as a matter of probability that there is a real and substantial risk to the life, not just the health, of the woman that can only be averted by the termination of the pregnancy.[3]

In 2009 the European Court of Human Rights (ECtHR) heard a case where the applicants alleged that Ireland breached their rights under the European Convention on Human Rights on the ground that, while abortion is lawful in very limited circumstances, Ireland failed to provide an effective and accessible procedure to enable women to determine if they qualified for a lawful termination in accordance with article 40.3.3.[4] The ECtHR found Ireland to be in violation of article 8 of the Convention (the right to private and family life) by failing to provide for this procedure.

Partially in response to the judgment from the ECtHR, the Protection of Life During Pregnancy Act 2013[5] was enacted, and it came into force in January 2014.[6] The Act restates the general prohibition on abortion in Ireland and regulates access to lawful termination of pregnancy in line with the Supreme Court case and the judgment from the ECtHR. The Act aims to protect human life during pregnancy and makes it a criminal offense to intentionally destroy unborn human life

---

[1] Protection of Life During Pregnancy Act 2013, No. 35 of 2013, http://www.irishstatutebook.ie/pdf/2013/en.act.2013.0035.pdf.

[2] IRISH CONSTITUTION (BUNREACHT NA HÉIREANN) art. 40.3.3, http://www.irishstatutebook.ie/en/constitution/.

[3] Attorney General v. X, [1992] I.R. 1, http://www.bailii.org/ie/cases/IESC/1992/1.html.

[4] A, B & C v. Ireland, [2010] E.C.H.R. 2032, http://hudoc.echr.coe.int/sites/eng/pages/search.aspx?i=001-102332.

[5] Protection of Life During Pregnancy Act 2013, No. 13 of 2013, http://www.irishstatutebook.ie/pdf/2013/en.act.2013.0035.pdf.

[6] DEPARTMENT OF HEALTH, IMPLEMENTATION OF THE PROTECTION OF LIFE DURING PREGNANCY ACT 2013: GUIDANCE DOCUMENT FOR HEALTH PROFESSIONALS ¶ 1.2 (2014), http://health.gov.ie/wp-content/uploads/2014/09/Guidance-Document-Final-September-2014.pdf.

except as provided in the statute.[7] It provides that a woman may obtain an abortion in Ireland if there is a risk of the loss of her life due to illness, emergency illness, or suicide.[8]

For termination due to a woman's illness, section 7 of the Act provides that two medical practitioners, one of whom must be an obstetrician and one a specialist doctor of a specialty that enables him or her to assess the risk of loss of the pregnant woman's life, must examine the pregnant woman and jointly certify the following:

> (i) that there is a real and substantial risk of loss of the woman's life from a physical illness, and
> (ii) in their reasonable opinion (being an opinion formed in good faith which has regard to the need to preserve unborn human life as far as practicable) that risk can only be averted by carrying out the medical procedure, and
> (b) that medical procedure is carried out by an obstetrician at an appropriate institute.

Section 8 provides that in emergency situations, a single doctor may make a certification and perform an abortion if certain prescribed circumstances are present.[9]

In cases where a real and substantial risk of loss of life is posed from the potential suicide of the woman, three medical practitioners (one obstetrician and two psychiatrists), in consultation with the woman's general practitioner where practicable and with the woman's consent, may certify that in their reasonable, honest, good-faith opinion, which regards the need to preserve the life of the fetus, the risk of the loss of the woman's life by suicide is real and substantial and can only be averted by a procedure that terminates the pregnancy.[10]

With respect to the gestational age of the fetus, the guidelines state that where certification has occurred there is no time limit imposed by the Act for terminating a pregnancy, but the responsible medical personnel will need to "use their clinical judgment as to the most appropriate procedure to be carried out, in cognisance of the constitutional protection afforded to the unborn, i.e. a medical or surgical termination or an early delivery by induction or Caesarean section."[11]

---

[7] Protection of Life During Pregnancy Act 2013, § 22, No. 13 of 2013.

[8] *Id.* §§ 7–9.

[9] *Id.* § 8.

[10] *Id.* § 9.

[11] DEPARTMENT OF HEALTH, *supra* note 6, ¶ 6.4.

Italy

Dante Figueroa
Senior Legal Information Analyst

Law 194 of 1978 legalized abortion in Italy.[1] The Law allows the voluntary interruption of pregnancy within the first ninety days of pregnancy, if the pregnancy, delivery, or maternity constitute a serious danger to the woman's physical or psychological health, taking into account her health, economic, social, or family situation; the circumstances under which conception occurred; and any diagnosis of anomalies or malformation of the unborn.[2] Abortion under these circumstances may be procured in a public health institution, regional health institution, or private clinic.[3] The consent of the unborn's biological father is not required.[4]

Abortion after the first ninety days of pregnancy is allowed in Italy in only two situations: (1) when the pregnancy or delivery involves a serious danger to the woman's life; and (2) when pathologies of the fetus are ascertained. In the latter case, those pathologies must consist of anomalies or malformations of the unborn that also create a serious danger for the physical or psychological health of the woman.[5] When there is a possibility that the child will survive outside of the womb, however, an abortion may only be carried out if the pregnancy or delivery pose a serious danger to the woman's health.[6] In such a case, the physician must take every appropriate measure to save the life of the child.[7]

The law requires a woman seeking an abortion to request an abortion in person.[8] In the case of women aged eighteen or younger the consent of those who exercise parental rights or guardianship over her is required.[9] However, during the first ninety days of pregnancy when there are reasons that impede or advise against consultation with such persons, or when after consultation these persons refuse their consent or are unable to reach a unanimous opinion, the attending medical personnel must request that a judge rule on the matter in a summary

---

[1] Legge 22 maggio 1978, n. 194, Norme per la tutela sociale della maternita' e sull'interruzione volontaria della gravidanza [Law No. 194 of May 22, 1978, Provisions on the Social Protection of Maternity and the Voluntary Interruption of Pregnancy], GAZZETTA UFFICIALE DELLA REPUBBLICA ITALIANA [G. U.] [OFFICIAL GAZETTE] No. 140 (May 22, 1978), http://www.normattiva.it/uri-res/N2Ls?urn:nir:stato:legge:1978-05-22;194.

[2] *Id.* art. 4.

[3] *Id.*

[4] *Id.* art. 5, paras. 1 & 2 (stating that the intervention of the father is only permitted "if the woman consents").

[5] *Id.* art. 6(b).

[6] *Id.* art. 7, para. 3, & art. 6(a).

[7] *Id.* art. 7, para. 3.

[8] *Id.* art. 12, para. 1.

[9] *Id.* art. 12, para. 2.

proceeding.[10]   In any case, if the treating physician ascertains the urgency of the need of an abortion, the physician is legally authorized to perform it.[11]

The request for an abortion to be performed on a woman who is incapacitated due to mental illness may be made by her guardian or her husband (unless legally separated),[12] but the woman must confirm the request.[13]

Except in the case of a medical emergency, the examining physician issues a certificate certifying the woman's pregnancy and her request for an abortion, and "invites" her to postpone her decision for seven days, after which period she may obtain an abortion.[14]

Medical personnel, including auxiliary staff, have the right to refuse to participate in abortion procedures by submitting a prior statement communicated to health authorities.[15] However, such objections are not permitted if the intervention is necessary to save the life of a pregnant woman who is in an imminent danger.[16]

The law punishes with imprisonment those who negligently cause a woman to have an abortion or a premature delivery,[17] those who cause an abortion through actions aimed at injuring the woman,[18] and those who perform an abortion without the woman's consent.[19] Additionally, the law punishes the woman and all those who cause or participate in an abortion without following the procedures established in the law.[20] However, women eighteen years of age or younger are exempted from criminal responsibility.[21]

---

[10] *Id.* art. 12, para. 3.

[11] *Id.*

[12] *Id.* art. 13, para. 1.

[13] *Id.* art. 13, para. 2.

[14] *Id.* art. 5, para. 4.

[15] *Id.* art. 9, paras. 1–3.

[16] *Id.* art. 9, para. 5.

[17] *Id.* art. 17.

[18] *Id.* art. 18, para. 2.

[19] *Id.* art. 18, para. 1.

[20] *Id.* art. 19, paras. 1–4.

[21] *Id.* art. 19, para. 6.

Latvia

Olena Yatsunska-Poff
Foreign Law Consultant

Abortion procedures are legal in Latvia. Such procedures are regulated under chapter 6 of the Sexual and Reproductive Health Law of February 19, 2002,[1] and Cabinet Regulation No. 590 on Organizational Procedures for the Termination of Pregnancy of October 28, 2003.[2]

Under law, abortion is legal if conducted during the first twelve weeks of the pregnancy[3] by a licensed gynecologist (childbirth specialist) at an inpatient medical treatment institution[4] upon the request of a woman, or in the case of a pregnancy resulting from rape.[5] Termination of pregnancy due to medical indications can be performed up to twenty-two weeks.[6]

An abortion procedure due to medical indications or in the case of a pregnancy resulting from rape is allowed only upon the written confirmation of the council of doctors and written consent of the woman. If a woman lacks the capacity to act, written consent of her guardian is required.[7] Written consent of at least one of patient's parents or a guardian is also required if a woman is under sixteen years of age.[8] Termination of a pregnancy for medical reasons or where the pregnancy resulted from rape is allowed if there is confirmation by the council of doctors or a certificate on a case of rape issued by a law enforcement institution. Parental consent in these situations is required for minor women.[9]

According to article 135 of the Latvian Criminal Code, unauthorized abortions are subject to prosecution. Performing abortions outside of a hospital, or at a hospital but without a legal basis, is prohibited. Such acts can be punished by varied terms of deprivation of freedom or community service, or a fine, with deprivation of the right to continue medical practice.[10] Performing an abortion against the will of a pregnant woman, or where the commission of an

---

[1] Seksuālās un Reproduktīvās Veselības Likums [Sexual and Reproductive Health Law] of Feb. 19, 2002, § 25, https://www.vestnesis.lv/ta/id/58982-seksualas-un-reproduktivas-veselibas-likums (official publication; in Latvian).

[2] Grūtniecības pārtraukšanas organizatoriskā kārtība [Organizational Procedures for the Termination of Pregnancy] No. 590 (prot. No. 56, 9.§) of Oct. 28, 2003, https://www.vestnesis.lv/ta/id/80585-grutniecibas-partrauksanas-organizatoriska-kartiba (official publication; in Latvian).

[3] *Id.* art. 26.2.

[4] *Id.* art. 26.4.

[5] Sexual and Reproductive Health Law art. 25.1.

[6] *Id.*

[7] *Id.* art. 26.3.

[8] *Id.* art. 27.2.

[9] *Id.* art. 27.3.

[10] CRIMINAL CODE OF THE REPUBLIC OF LATVIA art. 135, *available at* http://www.legislationline.org/documents/section/criminal-codes.

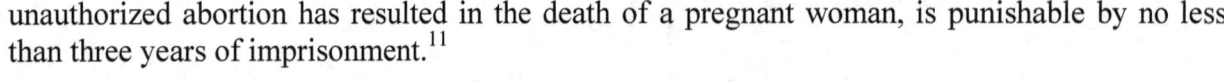

unauthorized abortion has resulted in the death of a pregnant woman, is punishable by no less than three years of imprisonment.[11]

---

[11] *Id.* art. 135.4.

Netherlands

Wendy Zeldin
Senior Legal Research Analyst

In the Netherlands abortions are available on request under the Law on the Termination of Pregnancy, but must be carried out by a physician in a hospital or a specially licensed clinic.[1] The gestational limit (none is stated in the Law) is said to be up to twenty-four weeks based on fetal viability,[2] but in any case clinics are said to "stick to 22 weeks."[3] There are also limits on the time period before which an abortion can be carried out: "not earlier than the sixth day after the woman has consulted the physician and on that occasion discussed her intention with him."[4] This consultation period begins to run when the woman's regular physician or an active specialist or family doctor of the woman's residence has referred her to a hospital or clinic; the physician must inform the woman whether he will provide her with the assistance at the latest within five days after the consultation and usually at the latest within three days.[5] In addition to consulting with the woman in person, the operating doctor must "advise her on the different options available" and "inform her of the medical risks"; minors (persons under eighteen years of age) must have parental consent.[6]

The Law provides for the issuance of administrative regulations "setting forth conditions governing the provision of assistance and the reaching of decisions designed to ensure that any decision to terminate a pregnancy is taken carefully and is reached only if the distress in which the woman finds herself leaves no other choice."[7] Such conditions are to ensure that the woman is given assistance and is well informed; that the physician is satisfied that the woman has made

---

[1] Wet van 1 mei 1981, houdende regelen met betrekking tot het afbreken van zwangerschap (Wet afbreking zwangerschap [Law on the Termination of Pregnancy]) (as last amended May 17, 2010, in force Oct. 10, 2010), § 2, http://wetten.overheid.nl/BWBR0003396/geldigheidsdatum_14-01-2015, available in English translation, as amended through Apr. 17, 2010, *at* http://www.hsph.harvard.edu/population/abortion/NETHERLANDS.abo.htm. The latter website also has an English translation of the Decree on the Termination of Pregnancy (May 17, 1984, as amended through May 18, 2009), implementing the Law.

[2] *Late zwangerschapsafbreking en levensbeëindiging bij pasgeborenen* [*Late Abortion and Euthanasia in Newborns*], RIJKSOVERHEID [GOVERNMENT OF THE NETHERLANDS], http://www.rijksoverheid.nl/onderwerpen/ levenseinde-en-euthanasie/late-zwangerschapsafbreking-en-levensbeeindiging-bij-pasgeborenen (last visited Jan. 14, 2015).

[3] Rutgers Nisso Groep, *The Netherlands*, *in* INTERNATIONAL PLANNED PARENTHOOD FEDERATION [IPPF] EUROPEAN NETWORK, ABORTION LEGISLATION IN EUROPE 57 (updated Jan. 2012), http://www.ippfen.org/sites/default/files/ Final_Abortion%20legislation_September2012.pdf.

[4] Law on the Termination of Pregnancy § 3(1).

[5] *Id.* §§ 3(2) & 3(3). However, the Law states, "[t]he period referred to in paragraph 1 shall be shortened by one day if the physician referred to in paragraph 2 takes three days after she has consulted him to inform her that he will not refer her." *Id.* § 3(4). If the physician does not give the woman a referral, "he shall immediately give her a dated written statement of this that in all cases shall mention the time at which she consulted him." *Id.* § 3(5).

[6] *Termination of Pregnancy in the Netherlands*, ANGLO INFO, http://southholland.angloinfo.com/information/ healthcare/pregnancy-birth/termination-abortion/ (last visited Jan. 15, 2014).

[7] Law on the Termination of Pregnancy § 5(1).

the abortion request "of her own free will, after careful consideration;" that the physician performs the operation "only if it can be considered justifiable on the basis of his findings;" and that after the pregnancy has been terminated, the women and those close to her "have access to adequate aftercare, including information regarding methods of preventing unwanted pregnancies."[8]

Termination of late-term pregnancies (those beyond twenty-four weeks), are governed by the Criminal Code[9] and by the Directions on the Non-Prosecution of Cases of Euthanasia and Late Abortions.[10] Under the Directions, late-term abortions are authorized in two instances involving serious fetal disorders: (1) the unborn has an untreatable disease expected to lead inevitably to its death during or immediately after birth; or (2) the unborn has a disease that has led to serious and irreparable impairment, where a (usually small) chance of survival exists.[11]

According to a Royal Dutch Medical Association publication, new measures are expected to be implemented in the spring of 2015 to clarify medical due diligence in connection with the evaluation of the suffering of newborns and dangers to the life of the woman when late-term abortions are performed.[12]

---

[8] *Id.* § 5(2).

[9] Wetboek van Strafrecht (Jan. 15, 1886, *as last amended effective* Jan. 1, 2015), §§ 82a (on the term "to take a life" including the killing of a viable fetus) & 296 (on criminal penalties for termination of pregnancy), http://wetten. overheid.nl/BWBR0001854/TweedeBoek/TitelXIXA/geldigheidsdatum_30-11-2014.

[10] Aanwijzing vervolgingsbeslissing levensbeëindiging niet op verzoek en late zwangerschapsafbreking [Directions on the Non-Prosecution of Cases of Euthanasia and Late Abortions] (in force Mar. 15, 2007), 46 STAATSCOURANT (Mar. 6, 2007), https://zoek.officielebekendmakingen.nl/Stcrt-2007-46-p10-SC79644.html.

[11] *Id.* §§ 4.1–4.3.

[12] Simone Paauw, *Regeling late zwangerschapsafbreking aangepast* [*Regulation of Late-Term Pregnancy Adapted*], MEDISCH CONTACT (July 10, 2014), http://medischcontact.artsennet.nl/Actueel/Nieuws/Nieuwsbericht/145670/ Regeling-late-zwangerschapsafbreking-aangepast.htm.

Norway

Elin Hofverberg
Foreign Law Research Consultant

Abortion in Norway is regulated by the Abortion Act.[1] Pursuant to that Act, abortions may be carried out before week twelve of the pregnancy at the request of the woman, unless strong health reasons speak against it.[2] Abortions after week twelve may only be performed if the pregnancy, delivery, or care for the child places the woman under an unreasonable physical or emotional burden;[3] the pregnancy, delivery, or care for the child places the woman in a difficult life situation;[4] there is a great risk that the child will suffer from a serious disease as a result of a genetic problem or problems encountered during the pregnancy;[5] the woman became pregnant after certain criminalized sexual abuse such as rape, underage sex, incest, etc.;[6] or she is suffering from serious depression or is seriously mentally challenged.[7]

Following week eighteen of the pregnancy, extraordinary grounds are required to justify an abortion.[8] If the fetus can live outside the womb permission for an abortion cannot be granted.[9] However, abortions carried out because of an immediate threat to the life and health of the woman as the result of continuing the pregnancy can be performed at any time during the pregnancy.[10]

Abortions can only be performed at the request of the pregnant woman herself.[11] If she is younger than sixteen such a request must be accompanied by permission from the county governor if her legal guardian (typically her parents) opposes the procedure.[12] A woman seeking an abortion must be informed both of the medical risks inherent in an abortion and the social support available to her.[13] There is no requirement that a woman have any ties to Norway in order to receive an abortion there.

---

[1] Lov om svangerskapsavbrudd [abortloven] Lov No. 50 of June 13, 1975, *as amended*, https://lovdata.no/dokument/ NL/lov/1975-06-13-50?q=abortlov.

[2] *Id.* art. 2.

[3] *Id.* art. 2, para. 3, item a.

[4] *Id.* art. 2, para. 3, item b.

[5] *Id.* art. 2, para. 3, item c.

[6] *Id.* art. 2, para. 3, item d.

[7] *Id.* art. 2, para. 3, item e.

[8] *Id.* art. 2, para. 6.

[9] *Id.*

[10] *Id.* art. 10.

[11] *Id.* art. 4.

[12] *Id.* art. 9.

[13] *Id.* arts. 1, 2, 5.

Abortions may only be performed by doctors.[14]   After week twelve, all abortions must be performed in a hospital.   Prior to week twelve, abortions may also be performed at other institutions approved by the county governor.[15]

Performing or aiding the performance of an abortion that violates the Abortion Act is penalized with a fine or three months' imprisonment.[16]

---

[14] *Id.* art. 3, para. 2.

[15] *Id.* art. 3.

[16] *Id.* art. 13.

Poland

Olena Yatsunska-Poff
Foreign Law Consultant

Under Poland's Act on Family Planning, Protection of the Human Fetus, and Conditions for Pregnancy Termination, an abortion procedure can be performed by a medical doctor only in cases where

- pregnancy is a threat to the life or health of the pregnant woman,

- prenatal examinations or other medical procedures indicate that there is a high probability of a severe and irreversible fetal defect or incurable illness that threatens the fetus's life, or

- there are reasons to suspect that the pregnancy is the result of an unlawful act.[1]

The termination of pregnancy is permitted during the first twelve weeks, when the fetus is incapable of living independently outside the body of the pregnant woman.[2]

The Act requires the written consent of the woman to terminate the pregnancy. In the case of a minor or fully incapacitated woman, the written consent of her legal representative is also required.[3]

According to the Penal Code, "whoever, with consent of the woman, terminates her pregnancy in violation of the law, or renders assistance to a pregnant women in terminating her pregnancy in violation of the law or persuades her to do so" is a subject to imprisonment for up to three years.[4] A longer term of imprisonment is prescribed for performing an abortion after the fetus is capable of living outside the pregnant woman's body.[5] The Penal Code provides for up to ten years of imprisonment for performing an abortion that causes the death of the pregnant woman.[6]

---

[1] Ustawa z Dnia 7 Stycznia 1993 of Planowaniu Rodziny, Ochronie Plodu Ludzkiego I Warunkah Dopuszczczalnosci I Przerywania Ciazu [Act on Family Planning, Protection of the Human Fetus, and Conditions for Pregnancy Termination] of Jan. 7, 1993, art. 4a1, DZIENNIK USTAW (official gazette) 1993, No. 17, Item 78, http://dziennikustaw.gov.pl/du/1993/s/17/78/1 (in Polish).

[2] *Id.* art. 4a.2.

[3] *Id.* art. 4a.4.

[4] KODEKS KARNY [PENAL CODE], Law of June 6, 1997, art. 152, § 1, *available at* http://www.legislationline.org/documents/section/criminal-codes/country/10 (in Polish; translation by author).

[5] *Id.* art. 152, § 3.

[6] *Id.* art. 154, § 1.

Portugal

Eduardo Soares
Senior Foreign Law Specialist

In Portugal, abortion is regulated by the Penal Code.[1] Article 142(1) of the Code determines that the termination of a pregnancy performed by a physician, or under the direction of a physician, in an official or officially recognized health establishment, and with the consent of the pregnant woman, is not punishable under the following conditions:

a) [Terminating the pregnancy] constitutes the only means of eliminating the danger of death or serious and irreversible damage to the body or the physical or mental health of the pregnant woman;

b) [An abortion] is indicated to avert the death [of the pregnant woman] or serious and lasting injury to [her] body or [her] physical or mental health, and is performed in the first 12 weeks of pregnancy;

c) There are reasons to believe that the unborn child will suffer from a serious, incurable illness or congenital malformation, and [the abortion] is performed within the first 24 weeks of pregnancy, except in the context of nonviable fetuses, in which case the interruption may be performed at any time;

d) The pregnancy resulted from a crime against sexual freedom and self-determination, and the abortion is performed in the first 16 weeks.

e) [The abortion] is performed, on the woman's volition, within the first ten weeks of pregnancy.[2]

The circumstances supporting the termination of a pregnancy must be verified by a medical certificate, written and signed before the abortion, by a physician different from the one who is performing or supervising the abortion.[3]

With regard to the conditions set forth in article 142(1)(a)–(d), the pregnant woman must provide her consent in a document signed by her, or at her request and, where possible, at least three days before the date of the abortion.[4]

When, in accordance with article 142(1)(e), the pregnancy is to be terminated within the first ten weeks, the pregnant woman must provide her consent in a document signed by her, or at her request, and delivered to the health facility at the time of the abortion. Before delivering her consent, the woman must undergo a period of reflection lasting a minimum of three days from

---

[1] CÓDIGO PENAL, Decreto-Lei No. 48/1995, de 15 de Março, http://www.pgdlisboa.pt/pgdl/leis/lei_mostra_articulado.php?tabela=leis&artigo_id=&nid=109&ficha=101&pagina=&nversao.

[2] *Id.* art. 142(1).

[3] *Id.* art. 142(2).

[4] *Id.* art. 142(4)(a).

the date she first consulted with a physician, who is responsible for providing her with access to information relevant to her making a free, conscious, and responsible decision.[5]

---

[5] *Id.* art. 142(4)(b).

Russian Federation

Peter Roudik
Director of Legal Research

The artificial termination of pregnancy in the Russian Federation is regulated under article 56 of Federal Law No. 323 of November 21, 2011, on Fundamentals of Citizens' Health Protection in the Russian Federation.[1] This Law establishes the basic principle that an abortion procedure can be conducted upon a woman's request during the first twelve weeks of pregnancy.[2] An abortion procedure can also be conducted during later stages of pregnancy depending on specific circumstances. The period for termination of a pregnancy can be extended up to twenty-two weeks if the pregnancy is the result of rape,[3] and it can be performed at any time because of medical conditions of a pregnant woman.[4] Since 2012, the performance of abortions because of a woman's difficult economic situation or other social reasons has been prohibited.[5]

Regulation No. 736 of December 3, 2007 (last amended Dec. 27, 2011) issued by the Russian Federal Ministry of Healthcare and Social Protection contains the list of medical reasons justifying termination of a pregnancy at any time.[6] The list includes tuberculosis, diabetes, cancerous tumors, varied heart diseases, and selected genetic and mental illnesses, among others. If a woman is under age fifteen, a pregnancy can be terminated before the fetus acquires the ability to live independently.[7] These government regulations prescribe the procedures for issuing permits for such abortions, as well as for abortions in cases where the pregnant woman has been recognized as legally incompetent and unable to express her own will.

The illegal performance of an abortion is prosecuted according to article 123 of the Russian Federation Criminal Code and is punishable with forced labor for a period of up to two years, or up to five years of imprisonment if an illegal abortion resulted in woman's death.[8]

---

[1] Fed. Law No. 323 of November 21, 2011, on Fundamentals of Citizens' Health Protection, ROSSIISKAIA GAZETA [ROS. GAZ.] (official publication), Nov. 23, 2011, http://www.rg.ru/2011/11/23/zdorovie-dok.html.

[2] *Id.* art. 56.

[3] Government Regulation No. 98 of February 6, 2012, § 1, ROS. GAZ., Feb. 15, 2012, http://www.rg.ru/2012/02/15/98-dok.html.

[4] Fundamentals of Citizens' Health Protection art. 56, § 4.

[5] Government Regulation No. 98, § 2.

[6] BIULLETEN' NORMATIVNYKH AKTOV FEDERALNYKH ORGANOV ISPOLNITELNOI VLASTI [BULLETIN OF FEDERAL EXECUTIVE REGULATIONS] (official gazette) Mar. 3, 2008, No. 9.

[7] *Id.*

[8] Criminal Code of the Russian Federation art. 123, ROS. GAZ., June 18–20, 25, 1996, *as amended.*

Spain

Graciela Rodriguez-Ferrand
Senior Foreign Law Specialist

According to Organic Law 2/2010 on Sexual and Reproductive Health and the Voluntary Interruption of Pregnancy, access to abortion in Spain is a woman's right.[1] Abortions may be legally performed within the first fourteen weeks of pregnancy at the woman's request, provided that the woman has been fully informed of her rights and about public benefits and assistance for maternal support, and has waited for a three-day period to pass between the provision of this information and the abortion procedure.[2]

Abortions may be legally performed up to twenty-two weeks for medical reasons

- after a prior medical assessment issued by a physician other than the one performing the abortion that the pregnancy poses a serious risk to the life or health of the woman (the assessment requirement may be waived in urgent cases);

- after a prior medical assessment issued by two specialist physicians other than the one performing the abortion that there is a serious risk of fetal abnormalities; or

- following the confirmation by a clinical committee of a report issued by a specialist physician other than the one performing the abortion that the fetus has abnormalities incompatible with life or an extremely serious or incurable illness.[3]

All abortion procedures must be performed by a specialist physician or under his or her direction in a public or accredited private hospital, with the written consent of the pregnant woman or her legal representative.[4] Parental consent is required only for girls younger than sixteen years of age. Girls aged sixteen and seventeen have access to abortion but are required to notify at least one parent or legal guardian. Notification is not required if the teen believes it would result in domestic violence, threats, coercion, abuse, or a situation of estrangement or helplessness.[5]

---

[1] Ley 2/2010 Orgánica de Salud Sexual y Reproductiva y de la Interrupción Voluntaria del Embarazo [Organic Law 2/2010 on Sexual and Reproductive Health and the Voluntary Interruption of Pregnancy] art. 3, BOLETÍN OFICIAL DEL ESTADO [B.O.E.] Mar. 4, 2010, http://www.boe.es/buscar/act.php?id=BOE-A-2010-3514.

[2] *Id.* art. 14.

[3] *Id.* art. 15.

[4] *Id.* arts. 13(Primero)–(Tercero).

[5] *Id.* art. 13(Cuarto).

Sweden

Elin Hofverberg
Foreign Law Research Consultant

Abortion in Sweden is regulated by the Abortion Act, which was most recently amended in 2013.[1] Pursuant to the Act, abortions may be performed before the expiration of the eighteenth week of pregnancy (also described as "eighteen weeks zero days") upon the woman's request, unless the procedure would cause serious risk to the woman's life or health.[2] Following week eighteen, a request for an abortion that specifies the "special reasons" justifying it must be presented to the National Board of Health and Welfare,[3] whose decisions cannot be appealed.[4] "Special reasons" include the physical and psychological impacts on the woman of continuing the pregnancy and/or the physical illness of the fetus. Subject to certain exceptions, such an application cannot be granted if the fetus is considered *Livsdugligt* (able to live outside the womb).[5] A fetus is currently considered *Livsdugligt* at twenty-two weeks and zero days.[6]

However, if continuing the pregnancy is associated with a serious threat to the woman's life or health, an abortion may be performed at any time during the pregnancy with the approval of the National Board of Health and Welfare.[7] In addition, if the threat to the woman is so serious that approval from the Board cannot be obtained in time, an abortion may be performed without the Board's approval and also need not be performed at a hospital.[8]

Only doctors may perform abortions[9] and abortions may only be performed at a general hospital or at other health institutions that the Social Care Inspectorate has approved, except as otherwise noted above.[10] The performance of abortions by nondoctors is criminalized. Punishment ranges from a fine to imprisonment for up to one year,[11] or up to four years if the crime is considered aggravated—for instance, if it has been done habitually or was meant as a threat to the woman's

---

[1] LAG OM ABORT [ABORTLAGEN] (Svensk Författningssamling [SFS] 1974:595), http://www.notisum.se/rnp/SLS/lag/19740595.htm.

[2] *Id.* art. 1.

[3] *Id.* art. 3.

[4] *Id.* art. 7.

[5] *Id.* art. 3, para. 2.

[6] STATENS OFFENTLIGA UTREDNINGAR [SOU] 2005:90 ABORT I SVERIGE: BETÄNKANDE AV UTREDNINGEN OM UTLÄNDSKA ABORTER, at 73, http://www.regeringen.se/content/1/c6/05/26/38/e9adc849.pdf.

[7] ABORTLAGEN art. 6.

[8] *Id.* art. 6, para. 2.

[9] *Id.* art. 5.

[10] *Id.* art. 5, para. 2.

[11] *Id.* art. 9.

life or health.[12] Licensed physicians who willfully violate provisions of the Act may face a fine or up to six months of imprisonment.[13]

A woman who has requested or undergone an abortion must be offered emotional support.[14]

As the result of a 2008 amendment to the Abortion Act,[15] women receiving an abortion in Sweden need not be Swedish or reside in Sweden.

---

[12] *Id.* art. 9, para. 2.

[13] *Id.* art. 10.

[14] *Id.* arts. 2, 8.

[15] LAG OM ÄNDRING I ABORTLAGEN (SFS 2007:998) (amending ABORTLAGEN, effective Jan. 1, 2008).

Switzerland

Wendy Zeldin
Senior Legal Research Analyst

Abortion under Swiss law is governed under Book Two, Specific Provisions, of the Criminal Code.[1] Abortion is exempt from penalty at any point in a pregnancy if, in a physician's judgment, the pregnancy must be terminated to prevent serious physical injury or serious psychological distress to the pregnant woman, and provided that the risk is "greater the more advanced the pregnancy is."[2] An abortion may also be performed at a pregnant woman's written request, if it is done by a licensed physician within twelve weeks of the start of the woman's last period and the woman "claims that she is in a state of distress."[3] The Law further provides that "the physician must have a detailed consultation with the woman prior to the termination and provide her with appropriate counselling."[4] In cases where the woman is incapable of judgment, her legal representative's consent is required.[5] Minors under the age of sixteen must see a counselor at a counseling service for adolescents, but "[p]arental consent (or information) is not required for minors capable of discernment (even if they are under 16). However, if a woman is under 16, usually the physician asks that one adult in the network of the young girl is informed about the abortion."[6]

---

[1] SCHWEIZERISCHES STRAFGESETZBUCH [STGB] [CRIMINAL CODE] Dec. 21, 1937 (status as of Jan. 1, 2015), SR 311, arts. 118–120, available in English translation *at* http://www.admin.ch/ch/e/rs/3/311.0.en.pdf (as of Jan. 1, 2015). Illegal abortion is covered under article 118 of the Code; contraventions by physicians of article 119 are covered under article 120.

[2] CRIMINAL CODE art. 119(1), http://www.admin.ch/ch/e/rs/311_0/a119.html.

[3] *Id.* art. 119(2).

[4] *Id.*

[5] *Id.* art. 119(3).

[6] SEXUAL HEALTH Switzerland, *Switzerland, in* INTERNATIONAL PLANNED PARENTHOOD FEDERATION [IPPF] EUROPEAN NETWORK, ABORTION LEGISLATION IN EUROPE 75 (updated Jan. 2012), http://www.ippfen.org/sites/default/files/Final_Abortion%20legislation_September2012.pdf.

Ukraine

Olena Yatsunska-Poff
Foreign Law Consultant

The artificial termination of pregnancy (abortion) in Ukraine is regulated under article 50 of Law No. 2801-XII of November 19, 1992, on Fundamentals of Ukrainian Legislation on Health Protection,[1] and under article 281 of the Civil Code of Ukraine No. 435-IV of January 16, 2003.[2] Both provisions are identical and establish that an abortion procedure can be conducted in certified medical establishments upon a woman's request during the first twelve weeks of pregnancy. In cases prescribed by legislation, abortions can also be performed from twelve to twenty-two weeks of pregnancy.[3]

A 2006 Decree of the Cabinet of Ministers of Ukraine specifies the list of circumstances that allow abortions to be performed during the twelve- to twenty-two-week period. These include illnesses that can threaten the life and health of the pregnant woman, such as diseases caused by fourth-stage HIV, tuberculosis, diabetes, and cancerous tumors; diseases of the blood and blood-forming organs; chromosomal diseases and malformation; dementia, mental diseases, and Alzheimer's disease; and nervous system and heart illnesses.[4] The Decree also allows a later-term abortion where the woman is under fifteen years of age or older than forty-five, and in instances where the pregnancy is the result of rape or may cause the woman to become disabled.[5]

The illegal performance of an abortion, which under Ukrainian law is the performance of abortion by a person who has no medical education, is prosecuted according to article 134 of the Ukrainian Criminal Code, and is punishable by imprisonment for up to two years.[6]

---

[1] Law No. 2801-XII of Nov.19, 1992 on Fundamentals of Ukrainian Legislation on Health Protection art. 50, http://zakon4.rada.gov.ua/laws/show/2801-12/page2 (official publication; in Ukrainian).

[2] Civil Code of Ukraine No. 435-IV of Jan.16, 2003, ch. 21, art. 281, § 6, http://zakon4.rada.gov.ua/laws/show/435-15/page6 (official publication; in Ukrainian).

[3] *Id.* art. 281, § 6.

[4] Decree of the Cabinet of Ministers of Ukraine No.144 of Feb.15, 2006, on the Realization of Article 281 of the Civil Code of Ukraine, http://zakon4.rada.gov.ua/laws/show/144-2006-п (official publication; in Ukrainian).

[5] *Id.*

[6] Criminal Code of Ukraine No. 2341-III of April 5, 2001, ch. 2, art. 134, http://zakon4.rada.gov.ua/laws/show/2341-14/page4 (official publication; in Ukrainian).

www.ingramcontent.com/pod-product-compliance
Lightning Source LLC
Chambersburg PA
CBHW080635290526
45790CB00007B/3077